YOUR FIRST 100

YOUR FIRST 100

How to Get Your First 100 Repeat Customers
(and Loyal, Raving Fans) Buying Your Digital
Products Without Sleazy Marketing or Selling
Your Soul

MEERA KOTHAND

"Making powerful marketing ideas simple and accessible so that solopreneurs and small business owners get clarity and cultivate a standout online brand presence minus the sleaze"

WWW.MEERAKOTHAND.COM

CONTENTS

You can download the First 100 Pack (with a
fillable PDF of the questions raised as well as
bonus resources) at
https://yourfirst100.com/bonus

INTRODUCTION – THE BIG, BOLD PROMISE

You could be thinking one of two things right now. Either...

A.   Seriously, just 100? That's barely going to get me the income I need! Sounds like a ridiculously low number; or

B. I'm struggling to get a *single* customer. How about we work on one first, and then I'll take it from there?

Whichever camp you're in, you're here because you have a digital product–based business or aspire to have one. You may already have an ecosystem of products or have none as yet. No matter how far along you are in your business, the idea of having repeat customers and loyal, raving fans buying *every single one* of your digital products is irresistibly tempting.

It has to be good, right?

Well, it is.

Repeat customers and loyal, raving fans are an asset to your business. The more you have, the better. If you have even a tiny inkling of doubt about this, here are some stats to show exactly why repeat customers are important.

Firstly, it is six to seven times more expensive to acquire a new customer than it is to keep a current one.[1] The probability of selling to a new prospect is 5 to 20%, while the probability of selling to an existing customer is **60 to 70%.**[2] On average, loyal customers are worth up to **ten times** as much as their first purchase.[3]

Let's get the definitions out of the way so that we're on the same page.

Who is a repeat customer and a loyal, raving fan?

Repeat customers and loyal, raving fans are people who are sold on whatever you sell because it's from *you* and they want it. You deliver *more* than a product to them. What they're buying into is the experience they know they'll get out of purchasing from you.

Their thought process could be

"I know she's going to make it simple and step by step."

"He's going to get me results and make it fun as well."

"I know I'm going to get so much more than what I paid for."

What you have on offer becomes *almost* insignificant to these buyers because they buy from you on principle. They have a set of expectations about the products you're selling even before knowing what they're buying into.

The key here though is **_not_** to reach 100—as counterproductive as that statement sounds because that's what you bought into with this book.

The number 100 just gives you an idea to wrap your head around.

The key here is to know *how* to nurture repeat customers and loyal, raving fans. Rather than look out for a single, once-off sale, you want to shift your thinking and convert each buyer or subscriber into a repeat, loyal customer.

If 100 is overwhelming, scratch that and think 10.

You could substitute 100 for whatever number you want. Because, if you know how to get to

100, you know how to get to 200, 300, and beyond.

This book isn't just about people who have already bought from you. Rather, it's about knowing how to cultivate and nurture people who *may* buy from you at some point—your subscribers, your website readers, your social media followers—and keep them coming back for more.

But what makes people buy again and again?

You could say they buy because they have a need. The product you're offering satisfies this need.

But is that *all* there is to buying?

What can you learn from the big brands, and how can you apply it to your digital product–based business?

Imagine the experience you get at an Apple store.

Or the experience you get when you shop at Target or Aldi.

Each of these places evokes a different buying experience. You immediately get a visual cue in your mind. You can almost feel the tangibility of the in-store experience.

People buy from a brand because of the way it makes them feel and the meanings attached to it.

But in an explosion of brands, does brand loyalty exist?

A recent survey done by Facebook suggests that brand loyalty is very much alive. Facebook found that 77% of people surveyed are returning to the same brands again and again, and 37% indicate that they make repeat purchases and are loyal to a company.[4] It's these brand loyalists that you want to nurture.

Brand Loyalists prioritize "more emotive and experiential qualities, like trust and service."[5] One of the standout words they use to describe the brands they love is "experience."

Experience covers all of the interactions a person has with a brand—products, website, delivery, customer service, right up to the cashier and more.

As an online business owner selling digital products, you need to pay attention to the experience your readers, subscribers, and buyers have with your brand too. Just like a brick and mortar business, your online business has several points of interaction with your audience. These brand interactions are called **touch points**.

In his book *What Customers Crave,*[6] Author Nicholas J. Webb defines five touch points: Pre, First, In, Core, and Post. In an article for *Harvard Business Review,*[7] Author Adam Richardson defines touch points as Setting, Messages, Interactions, and Products. So there are variations in terminology, but the idea behind what a touch point is, is the same.

In this book, I'll introduce you to the **5P Touch Framework**:
1. Pre-Touch Point
2. Premier (First) Touch Point
3. Pivotal Touch Point
4. Prime Touch Point
5. Post Touch Point

Let's see how these play out for a brick and mortar store before you see how they translate to an online digital product–based business.

Imagine you're buying a car at the dealership.

You start with the **pre**-touch point. At this stage you have not interacted with the car dealership before. You may have received some marketing material. Or you may have heard a friend mention the fabulous service they received.

The **premier** (first) touch point happens when you call in, and the receptionist is this really nice and helpful lady who even lets you in on when the best sales rep will be around to serve you. Or maybe one of the sales staff greets you at the door with a warm smile and shows you to your seat.

The **pivotal** touch point is when the salesperson tries to understand the needs you have for your car. She engages with you and shows a genuine interest in your life. She asks you how many kids you have and how much space do you need. She empathizes with your long commute to work. She shows you that she understands the problems you have and assures you she has the perfect solution.

The **prime** touch point is how she takes you through the sales process right up till delivery of your new car keys. Does she have answers to all your questions? Does she support you through the buying process? Does she dispel doubts and objections you have? Does she calm your fears and reassure you that you're making the right choice? Does she walk you through the features and benefits of the car and invite you for a test drive? The sale is made when all of these needs are met.

The **post** touch point is the after sales service you receive. Does the dealership offer free servicing as part of their sales package? How do the workers greet you when you come for your first service?

Now, imagine if one of these touch points disintegrates...

What if the staff member who helps you arrange your first complimentary service is downright rude? The warm greetings you received prior to the sale are gone.

Or what if the team servicing your car makes you wait for three hours even though you have an appointment? They then hand over your car without even an apology?

How does that make you feel?

Ruins the excitement you felt before, right?

Makes you doubt they care about service standards or their customers. You may even question buying from them again.

That's what happens when a brand experience is inconsistent across touch points.

Businesses create a brand experience for the customer through these various touch points. Each touch point builds on the next to create a holistic compelling experience.

It's not a singular thing but an accumulation of things that create an experience. ***But how in the world will this help you get 100 repeat customers buying your digital products? Why does it even matter?***

Because your online business is just as tangible as a physical store.

Just because you run a business online doesn't mean you neglect experience from your brand equation. Your brand should feel the same to your audience every time they interact with it.

As an online business owner, here's potentially how someone comes into contact with your brand.

Pre-touch point is where they have not yet engaged with your paid products. Someone tagged you in a Facebook group, and they hear about you. You piqued their curiosity with a pin image on Pinterest, and they clicked through to arrive on your site. They may have heard about you on a podcast. A peer or friend may have mentioned your site. Every one of these contributes to a pre-touch point moment.

Premier (First) touch point is the first direct touch point they have with your brand. This is where they usually sign up for an incentive or lead magnet on your site and go from a casual reader to a subscriber. They have chosen to give you permission to contact them at this stage. Other examples of first touch point moments are your welcome email, thank you pages, one-time offer pages, an online inquiry they send in, or an on-site chat feature.

Pivotal touch point is when they are actively engaging with you via your content, email sequences, webinars, and any subscriber exclusive content. I call it pivotal because this is the touch point which does a lot of the heavy lifting for you. Some people may develop the "know-like-trust" factor with you and your brand within the first two touch points above, but the majority will not. So for most of your audience, this touch point is largely responsible for whether someone goes on to make their first purchase from you or not.

Prime touch point is everything that happens just before and after purchase. Your checkout system, your welcome onboarding for buyers, if the expectation of the product is met, and the level of support they receive are all examples of prime touch point moments.

Post Touch Point is how you make your customers feel post-purchase. How do you delight them? How do you solicit testimonials and reward feedback? Do you offer continuous after sales support? These are examples of post touch point moments.

An online digital product–based business with 100 repeat customers and the potential to grow further has a **singular brand footprint burned into every single touch point**—right from pre-touch point to post. A consistent experience is comforting and makes it very hard for customers to go elsewhere once they're hooked on to your brand. At the same time, when experience differs from one touch point to another, customers lose trust.

Sue Cockburn, CEO of Growing Social Biz, says that "Customers want to have confidence that we'll deliver on our promises every time, not just when it's convenient. In fact, if we consistently deliver good products and services across our organization, if we mean what we say and say what we mean, if we underpromise and overdeliver, the potential for our organization to not only grow but reach extraordinary heights is real. It won't guarantee success but it will lay the foundation for us to achieve more and it will usually separate us from our competitors."[8]

Here's a visual representation of how the 5P Touch Framework looks like for online digital product–based businesses.

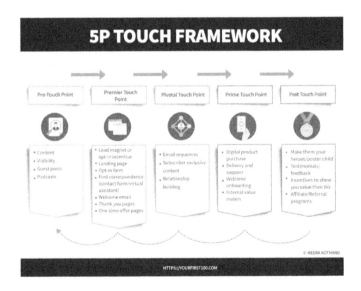

Before you freak out about how alien this whole concept sounds—how overwhelm-

ing and intimidating this diagram looks—
take a deep breath.

I bet you're already creating these touch points.

You probably have a site. You may even have an opt-in form where you're inviting readers to sign up. You may even have something for sale.

We're just giving a name to the flows that your audience and customers are already experiencing at different points.

For now, you don't need to know anything beyond being aware that there are five touch points and that you may already be creating several of these.

How this book will help you build a business of repeat customers and loyal, raving fans

This book will introduce you to a system of ideas and questions you need to think about, ask yourself, and apply to your online business in five core areas.

These core areas are

• Brand

- Content
- Email Marketing
- Digital Products (and Offers)
- Selling Practices

It's these core areas which anchor and impact your touch points. How you deal with them determines whether your business has the capacity to attract repeat customers and loyal, raving fans.

Why these five?

Because these are the five which have the most potential for growth and impact on your online business. These are also the areas where I've seen most of my clients and readers doing things differently.

There will be questions at the end of each section.

There will be lots of thinking.

There will be light bulb moments.

There may even be frustrations because of all the gaps you uncover.

But will doing this get you more engagement from your audience? YES.

Will doing this potentially bring you more income? That's the plan!

Ground rules?

Just two.

One—Give yourself grace and time.

This book is a process and framework for what you need to optimize and the steps you need to take to get your first 100 repeat customers and beyond.

It *will* take time.

Heck, building a loyal brand does—online or offline. As you inch closer to the end, you *will* start to see how it all comes together.

Two—Do the work.

You know which of these core areas you need more help with. Go ahead and skip to what you need help with the most.

Don't feel like going through all the questions at the end of each section? Don't. But do them for those areas you feel you need more help with.

You may be familiar with or even to a certain extent be doing the things I'll cover. But it's about knowing how to do it *right*.

That's the difference between any other online business and *yours*.

YOURS which is positioned to attract repeat customers and loyal, raving fans.

If you're ready, let's go!

———>**Your First 100 Pack** has a set of additional resources to help you through the exercises. Download it for free at **https://yourfirst100.com/bonus.**

SECTION 1
A Brand That Paves the Way for Your First 100 Repeat Customers and Loyal, Raving Fans

I was three months into my business when I sent out my first survey. I had a list of about 500 people whom I was emailing consistently. Two of the responses in the survey jolted me.

They read: *I like your brand.*

What does having a brand mean to an online business owner like you?

Here's a quote by Jeff Bezos, CEO of Amazon: "Your **brand** is what other people say about you when you're not in the room."

Your brand is your reputation, and it lives in the minds of your audience. It's what your audience says it is, **not** what you say it is.

But you *can* guide and influence what people think about your brand through intentional actions.

You don't need a brand strategist to get started with branding. In this section, you'll discover the principles and ideas behind having a brand that paves the way for your first 100.

1 – WHY DOES BRAND MATTER?

As humans, we have a natural tendency to sort, label, and categorize.

It helps us make sense of our world.

We give people tags based on the most dominant attribute that comes across to us.

Likewise, every personal brand comes with a set of emotions and attributes attached to it.

How does your ideal customer see your brand?

What do they think about and what do they feel when they hear your name or see a piece of your content?

Do they see you as fun?

Responsive?

Honest?

Detailed?

All of these are good attributes, but you can't be all of them.

Meera Kothand is not a fun brand. That doesn't mean I'm bland and boring. It's just that I choose not to lead my brand with the "fun" attribute.

You choose what attribute you lead your brand with.

So if you're fun, you're fun all over.

This extends across every point of interaction with your audience from the pre-touch point to the post touch point.

Now, let's relate this to something we're all familiar with—food.

Just like mom's cooking

Just like grandma's

I bet you've seen food brands from canned soup to pasta sauce to restaurants using these slogans in their advertising.

Ever wondered why?

That's because mom's and grandma's cooking brings to mind a certain emotional experience.

For many of us, this also involves sensory cues. Whether that's the familiar smell of spices, home-baked bread, or chicken broth depending on the type of food we grew up with.

By using that slogan, the brands try to tap into the emotional experience we associate with mom's or grandma's cooking. It gives their products character, and the emotions we attach to home cooking rub off on their product.

If the product delivers on the experience it promises, then the brand has placed its footprint and stake on that set of attributes.

Your brand strategy is where you tell people how you want your brand to be perceived—by the content you write, and the visual and verbal cues you use. You tell your audience what you want to be known for.

Your audience takes direction from you.

But to do that you need to be clear about your brand attributes.

What are the emotions and personality traits of your brand?

What vibe do you want your brand to give off?

What words do you want people to associate with your brand?

If you run your business under your name, then your brand is you. But, if your business is under another name, think of that brand as a person. How will you present that brand to your readers? How will you describe that person?

The biggest branding sin is deciding on your color palette and logo before deciding on your brand strategy.

This is like taking a road trip without a map. Your bells and whistles—colors, logos, and images—need to align with your brand attributes, not the other way around. For instance, you may make a conscious decision not to use gold, flowers, or jewelry on your images, no matter how trendy they are, because they simply do not fit your brand.

A well thought out brand strategy gives your business clarity. It acts like a beacon and tells you exactly how you're supposed to be across each of the touch points. It also makes it easy for anyone you work with—VAs, designers—to get on the same page quickly.

In the exercise at the end of this section, you'll have examples of descriptor words to pick from. But you don't have to be limited to those words. Use a thesaurus and narrow it down to 3–5 words that form the core of your brand. It's these words that influence your brand vibe, your tone, your voice, and even the audience you attract.

2 – YOU'RE NOT FOR EVERYBODY

You don't sell your products to everybody.

Of course, you're free to do so.

But you don't actively attract everyone. You only spend your time and resources attracting your ideal customer.

This person is someone who you love to work with and serve. If you had a "poster boy or girl" for your brand, this would be them. Often, it's your style that attracts these people.

What type of person would you absolutely love to serve?

Who would benefit the most from what you offer?

And whom would you love to see represent your brand's ideal customer?

Imagine this person or if you have an existing customer like this, get ready to sketch this person out in as much detail as you can at the end of this section.

Knowing who these people are in your business will help you make better decisions about your offer which includes the promises or outcomes, how you package your digital product, and pricing, as well as the language you use on your sales page.

Remember that these are the people you want to actively market to. We'll refer to them as your ideal customer from here on.

Let's pause for a second now.

This is a question I often get asked.

But what if I have more than one type of ideal customer?

That's perfectly fine.

The big brands often market to different customer segments—single working moms, empty nesters, mompreneurs, tech-savvy millennials.

As a solopreneur and small business owner, you don't have the capacity to target so many different customer segments. It's ideal to focus on 1–2 segments at most so that you can focus on speaking the right language to the right customer because each segment will have different triggers that make them buy.

But, here's the thing. The brand attributes that we spoke about have to attract your ideal customer. If you think of your brand as confident and powerful and your target audience is girly and feminine, then you either have to rethink your ideal customer or your brand attributes.

If you're building your business from scratch, you can mold your brand as you grow. It's just like molding a piece of clay. But if your business has been around for some time and you've already built up a small-to-sizable audience, you need to consider if your ideal customer sees you the same way as you'd like to be seen? If your answer is no, you have to ask yourself where the disconnect happens?

Is it your voice? Your visuals? Your copy?

Then take steps to bridge the gap.

It *will* take time to realign your brand. You may even end up losing people who don't gel with your new brand direction. But it's the best decision for your brand and business in the long run.

3 – CARVE A SPACE FOR YOUR STAKE

We can't talk about branding without discussing the competition.

Your competition is anyone who operates in the same niche as you. This is something that I've always told my readers:

Quit trying to be better than your competitors. Think of how you can position yourself differently.

Because when you do, you pretty much eradicate the competition.

Knowing who the other players in your niche are will help you articulate your brand message clearly.

What vibes do their brands give off?

Can you find out who they're attracting by the way they look and sound?

What messages are they trying to convey and what do they offer?

Have a look at their home page, their visuals, and their writing to find clues.

Are the brand attributes that you picked—your brand, personality, and vibe— distinct from those of your competitors? Can you put a stake in the ground for them or have they already been taken?

Your ideal customer needs to see how you're different. You help him/her see this by finding that white space and putting your stake in it.

Once you do, you won't ever fear that your competition has similar products or content to yours because you know that you target different markets and buyers who want different things.

Once you've determined the essence of your brand and know where it stands in relation to others in your space, you need to verbalize its benefits.

This is what we call an elevator pitch or a core positioning statement.

Start by writing down 1–3 main benefits your brand offers your ideal customer. You want to stick with 1–3 of the most compelling and important benefits that will make people sit up and take notice.

Anything more than that and you lose attention.

What does your ideal customer **gain** from doing business with you? What are the advantages of doing business with you?

Clarity? Confidence? More profits? Less stress?

For example, if you're a sleep therapist for parents with toddlers and you offer consulting, your core benefit isn't that you help children sleep through the night.

So what if they do?

Your core benefit is that you help your ideal customer (parents) feel less stressed. You ease their tension. Bedtime doesn't have to turn into a battlefield.

"I reply to emails within 24 hours" is not a benefit.

It's what you do.

You need to communicate *why* that 24-hour turnaround even matters to your ideal customer.

A beautifully designed course workbook is not a benefit.

It's a feature. It's what you sell or offer.

But why does what you sell or offer matter to them?

Keep digging into the benefit and don't get stuck on the features of what you do.

What is that one core thing that sets you apart from other businesses? What is different about the way you do things?

Now put it into a hook or core positioning statement.

What you do - Who you help - Your benefit

I make powerful marketing ideas simple and accessible for solopreneurs and small business owners so that they get clarity and cultivate a standout online brand presence minus the sleaze.

I teach female creatives how to organize and declutter their homes so that they get unstuck physically, creatively, and emotionally. They go on to feel more emotional balance and less stress.

Look at your positioning statement.

Is it different from the other players in your space?

Is this what helps your ideal customers the most and helps you stand out?

If so, you've got a winner!

This, together with your brand attributes, will guide your copy, your visuals, and your tone.

It'll also help you communicate your brand when you actively make an effort to be known, liked, and trusted by your audience.

4 – THE KNOW-LIKE-TRUST FORMULA

Know, Like, and Trust are three words that are loosely thrown around.

But what exactly do they mean?

There are a lot of interconnections between Know, Like, and Trust. To a certain degree, you can't have one without the other.

Let's start with **KNOW**.

In a TED talk, Brené Brown said: "In order for connection to happen, we have to allow ourselves to be seen—really seen." [9]

Getting your audience to KNOW you starts with being visible. When you're trying to grow your business, being seen matters.

I was chatting with a friend of mine who also runs an online business and she said, "Meera, you're everywhere. I need to take a course from you on visibility."

I was able to get noticed when I was brand new to the online space because I was featured on podcasts, summits, and interviews. I also guest posted for sites like Smart Blogger, MarketingProfs, Addicted2Success, and several others.

When you get featured on a platform bigger than yours, with more social proof and a bigger audience, some of that rubs off on you. Your credibility quotient skyrockets and people start to take notice.

Even if you already have an existing audience, are you actively seeking out opportunities to get visible? Because people can't buy from you if they don't know you exist.

Getting your audience to **LIKE** you starts with being open to a conversation, being approachable, and being helpful. My friend Kirsten Oliphant from Create If Writing is a huge advocate of email marketing, and I love what she says about responding personally to emails: "I like to say in some of my signup email sequences that until I'm Taylor Swift, I will respond if they reply to my emails."[10]

That's not to say you should be chained to your desk for hours responding to emails. But with increasing automation, the brands that stand out are the ones that take an interest in their audience.

In his book *Top of Mind*,[11] Author John Hall compares **TRUST** to making a campfire. You can't start it and leave, expecting it to continue burning. The fire needs a constant supply of oxygen. You need to fan the flame and add more wood. You need to constantly see what needs to be done to keep the flame going.

The same is true about building trust. You can't publish a 5,000-word article that your audience adores, garner thousands of shares, and then go silent for months without publishing another piece.

This isn't to say you publish low-quality posts five times a week. That's silly.

You need to communicate with your audience consistently and deliver content through a channel that works for you and them. We'll discuss content more in the next section.

But trust doesn't extend to content alone. It extends to email marketing, your products and services, as well as the way you communicate and engage with your audience.

The tone you use in your emails can't be girly or snarky when your brand is supposed to be empathetic and professional. You can't say your brand is minimalist, budget conscious, or frugal when the affiliate products you promote send a different message.

This is when your audience starts to lose trust in your brand.

Do you see how the core of your brand extends and influences every decision you make for your business?

Do you see how it impacts your touch points?

You can't look at them as isolated stand-alone components if you want to build a business of 100 or more repeat, loyal customers.

This section is the foundation for how you deal with the other core areas. You may have considered optimizing your email marketing strategy, your products, your content, as well as your selling practices, but your core—your brand—has to influence each of those areas.

In the next section, we'll discuss the specific role of content in your pathway to repeat sales and customers. Now, have a look at the questions below. Remember that you can download all of these, together with extra resources, in a fillable PDF at **https://yourfirst100.com/bonus**.

ACTION

It's easy to say I'm working on my branding without knowing what that actually means. So let's work on the branding that will lead you to that loyalty recipe.

1. Brainstorm a list of all the adjectives or emotions that describe your brand. These are your brand attributes. Write these down and then trim the list until you have 3–5 that communicate the personality and essence of your business.

If you're struggling with this exercise, think of brands that you are loyal to. Think about authors and musicians. Or your favorite tech companies. Once you get comfortable with this exercise, think of brands you are loyal to in the online space. That could be Marie Forleo, Mark Manson, or Gary Vaynerchuk. What words come to your mind when you think about these personal brands? Then attempt the exercise again and apply it to your own brand.

Adventurous	Artistic	Authoritative
Analytical	Authentic	Bold

Bright
Bubbly
Calm
Candid
Caring
Casual
Charming
Cheerful
Chic
Clear
Colorful
Compassion-
ate
Conservative
Dangerous
Daring
Delightful
Detailed
Down-to-
earth
Dynamic
Edgy
Elegant
Energetic
Exciting

Expert
Feminine
Flirty
Frank
Friendly
Fun
Genuine
Girly
Honest
Humorous
Informal
Inspiring
Intense
Kind
Knowledge-
able
Motivating
Optimistic
Out-of-the-
box
Outspoken
Overdeliver
Playful
Powerful

Practical
Quirky

Rebellious
Regal
Savvy
Silly
Simple
Smart
Snarky
Sophisticat-
ed
Spiritual
Strong
Stylish
Thoughtful
Trustworthy
Unique
Upbeat
Warm
Whimsical
Wise
Witty

2. What can your readers depend on you to do? Can they depend on you to lift them up or motivate them? Can they depend on you to provide detailed technical how-tos? This doesn't have to be just one thing. It could be a set of things that form the core of your brand.

3. How do you want customers to talk and feel about your brand?
If you already have an audience, look out for cues as to what they're saying. What do they say in their emails to you? What do they say in their comments?

4. Do customers define your brand in the same way you do? Is there a gap? What do you need to do differently so that your audience feels more of the emotions that you want them to feel?

5. Who is your ideal customer? What makes you drawn to working with him or her? Try and get as detailed as you can. Find a royalty-free stock photo to represent him or her. The questions or prompts below will help you understand at a deeper level the type of person you want to attract and influence. It will give you insight into their worries, stresses, and frustrations.

Are they male or female?
Are they married or single?
Do they have children? How many?
What does he/she want to achieve in the next year?
What does he/she want to achieve in the next 3 years
What worries does he/she have?
Where does he/she hang out on social media?
What interests/hobbies does he/she have?
What does he/she care about?
What does he/she despise?
What does he/she believe is stopping her/him?

If you don't have access to an audience or your business is still new, it may be tough getting answers to these questions. If so, you may need to get answers from other sites like Alexa or SimilarWeb. Here's a post I wrote that shows you step by step how you can find information about your ideal audience when you don't have direct access to them yet: http://meera.tips/reader-profile.

6. Who is your competition? How are you different? What is unique about your brand and how do you stand out from others in your niche?

7. What are the benefits you offer and why do they matter? What do customers gain from doing business with you? Write out your core positioning statement.

SECTION 2
Content That Paves the Way for Your First 100 Repeat Customers and Loyal, Raving Fans

Most of us think of the buying process as linear.

You sell something, and your ideal customer buys it.

But often it looks like one big scribble.

There is nothing linear or predictable about the route someone takes to a sale. And people aren't always ready to buy the first time you launch an offer. That doesn't mean that they'll never be interested.

When they say no to your offer, it often means a **"not right now."**

Not a **"not ever**."

People's decisions are often triggered by a lot of external factors—financial, personal, or business—which are out of your control.

It's interesting to reference a study by Everett Rogers. His research[12] states that people fall into five different personality types when it comes to taking up any new innovation:

1. Innovators
2. Early Adopters
3. Early Majority
4. Late Majority
5. Laggards

While this study refers to technology, you can see how it could relate to digital products.

There are people who will jump at the opportunity to buy a product that's pre-selling, and there are those who simply won't. I'm the latter.

So your product idea isn't necessarily broken when people don't buy the first time.

Someone could go from reader to buyer all in a single day.

Someone else could take three months.

I had someone on my email list make her first purchase a full year later.

According to Brian Carroll, Author of *Lead Generation for the Complex Sale,*[13] almost 95% of your audience or subscribers are not ready to buy. But 70% of them will *eventually* buy from you or your competitors.

This is where content comes into play.

You score with your content marketing if that 70% think of you and come to you when they're ready.

They may be ready tomorrow, a year later, or two years later.

Your part in the process is to be present, cultivate trust, and build a relationship with them through content. Your ideal customer rewards you with loyalty and the sale if you prove your value in the form of content *before* the sale. In this section, you'll discover the specific principles and ideas behind content that paves the way for your first 100.

5 – THE CONTENT CHAIN LINK

There are various stages that an ideal customer goes through when they come into contact with your brand.

Here's what the typical journey is like for an ideal customer:

> Stranger > Casual reader > Subscriber > Engaged subscriber> Customer > Brand advocate

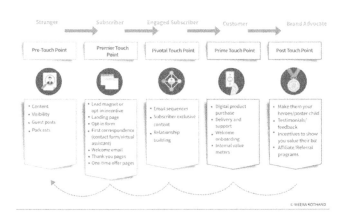

If you look closely, it nicely aligns with the 5P Touch Framework.

Existing customers who know, like, and trust you have a different relationship with you than a brand-new subscriber who doesn't know you yet.

Matching the right content to where your audience is on their journey with you is critical to helping them move forward.

Let's look at the different content pieces you need to create to fully capitalize on each touch point.

Pre-Touch Point

The content you will create at this stage is about becoming visible. We discussed this in section 1 on building Know-Like-Trust. This is where you create content and engage in activities that will get people on to your site.

This person has absolutely no clue about you, so you need to promote yourself and your content through external channels like guest posts, podcasts, and social media. Your headline and call to action in your author bio or podcast pitch are promises of the type of content they can expect if they click through. If you keep those promises, your reader will be ready to take the next step.

Premier (First) Touch Point

This is where a casual reader is ready to become a subscriber. But you need to **invite** them to become a subscriber. This is where you offer a compelling lead magnet or opt-in incentive. Your site also has to be optimized and prepared to convert a casual reader to a subscriber.

Pivotal Touch Point

I like to say that the magic happens when someone is already on your list. This is where you create content to give them a deeper glimpse into your values and teachings. This is where you nurture them through regular emails and sequences.

The content I share in my pivotal touch point is distinct from the content I share on my blog. While my blog posts cover "How-tos," my email content shares strategies, is thought-provoking, and gives a glimpse behind the workings of my business.

This is intentional.

A subscriber is special because they're deeper in the relationship, and if you nurture them right, they go on to become a buyer. Content here has the potential to be transformational but only if you let it. We'll cover how you can use email marketing to cultivate repeat customers and loyal, raving fans in section 3.

Prime Touch Point
Now that you have engaged subscribers, what type of content will encourage them to become customers? Prime content pieces should nudge and guide your ideal customer through the buyer's journey.

At any given time, most of your ideal customers will fall into one of these five categories.

Category 1: They have no idea about the problem that your product or service solves or why it needs to be solved in the first place.

Category 2: They are becoming aware of the problem that your product or service solves. They still have a lot of questions. But you've got their attention, and they are starting to trust you.

Category 3: They are aware of the problem that your product or service solves. They trust you and love your content. Often, they feel the product is right for them, but they're not quite ready to buy.

Category 4: They are ready to buy, but they have questions.

Category 5: They've purchased. They are ready for more good stuff from you.

You want to move people from Category 1 through to Category 5. You want to build a relationship with your ideal customer by empowering and educating them with content so that they inch toward your solution. Your role is to be top of mind when they're ready to purchase.

This is why building a pool of content surrounding your products is important because different pieces of content will appeal to different readers depending on where they're at in the journey toward your solution.

Let's take a look at how to put this into practice with a real example.

I'll show you how I build content pieces surrounding my program "Product in 7." Each one of these proposed content pieces can be a blog post, video, email, or any other content medium. This is a process that I talk about in greater detail in my book The One Hour Content Plan.

Core problem that the program solves: Overwhelm from course creation. Fear that digital product won't sell.

Promise of the offer: Create a tiny digital product that sells in 7 days.

What does someone need to be aware of before purchasing your product?
If they don't know they have a problem to be solved in the first place, they won't appreciate your solution. Some may be aware, and some may not be. You need to raise awareness of the core problem so that they recognize it. Here's what your audience may be struggling with:

- Thinking that their first product has to be a course when it doesn't

- Undermining the potential of small products to make money

- Thinking that creating products is a painful, long-drawn-out affair when it doesn't have to be

What content will get your ideal customer's attention? This is where you raise awareness that they have a problem that has to be solved:

- 13 things killing the sales of your product

- Every single mistake I made with launching digital products

- Why your course is killing that sale

What raises interest in your solution:

- 33 things nobody tells you about launching and creating a product

- The 7-step process to creating a digital product in 7 days

- 7 products you can create that are not a course

- When does marketing for your product start?

What raises desire for your solution:

- How to create and launch products that sell out every. single. time

Each one of these pieces builds on the last and contributes to the pool of content surrounding the offer. They give a potential buyer a clearer picture of your offer and what it does. It supports them through the buying process.

Post Touch Point
Once they buy, how do you support them with content post-purchase? Post-purchase type content pieces could be a welcome onboarding sequence, a Facebook group, a Slack channel, live calls, special buyers only workshops, etc.

Now, ask yourself where your content possibly falls short. In which areas—Pre, Premier (First), Pivot, Prime, and Post—does your content fall short? Because if you have content missing at any one step, you have a lost opportunity.

You won't be able to pull readers through the length of their journey and convert them to a brand advocate and customer.

6 – DOES YOUR CONTENT DE-MAND ATTENTION?

Attention is the currency of the web, right?

Your brand doesn't have to be bright or flashy. The words you use can be subtle and not loud. You can be an introvert.

Regardless of all of this, does your content still attract attention?

But not just attention.

Are you able to get your audience to take action on that content and at the same time turn that attention to business growth?

That's what matters.

Content that has the potential to get attention, inspire action in your ideal customer, and contribute to your business growth has to add to the literature in your niche and not to the noise.

Value doesn't come from feeding your audience with free tips that everyone else is already saying. You provide value when you're able to inspire a commitment to change. You add to the content literature in your niche when you have a distinctive point of view. This is also how you build content authority.

In *Content Inc.*, Author Joe Pulizzi [14] calls this the "content tilt." The content tilt is what will separate you from everyone else in your niche. The content tilt is what makes you and your content different. This is what will get your audience to take notice of you and reward you with their attention. There are a few ways you can find your own tilt.

- What questions are your audience members asking that aren't addressed in your niche?

- What perspectives and viewpoints in your niche do you oppose or take an opposite view on?

- What is everyone saying that isn't necessarily true?

- Are there any specific methods you use that get your readers/clients results?

- What are common misconceptions readers have about the content in your niche or what mistakes do they make?

- What are your biggest light bulb moments that have impacted the way you do certain things and how you help your readers or clients?

All of these are questions you can ask yourself to help you figure out your own "content tilt." Because once you've figured out your "tilt," it's easier for you to put a stake in the ground and claim it.

To get 100 repeat, loyal customers buying your products, your ideal customer needs to associate you with the topic of your offer. If you regularly publish posts, speak on podcasts, do guests posts, or share on a particular topic, you get associated with that topic.

When you consistently deliver quality content and you go deep and narrow rather than wide and shallow, you're sending a message to your audience. You're showing them that you have knowledge and expertise in that particular topic.

It also gets easy for your audience to tag you in social media conversations. When people ask for help in Facebook groups on a specific topic, your ideal reader should be able to tag you as the "go-to" person for that topic.

But if you write on a whole range of topics, and your content doesn't have a thread through it, you make it hard for your audience to associate you with anything. This is where you start to send mixed messages. It's easier to convince your ideal customer to buy from you when your products and offers are on a topic where you're seen to have expertise or authority.

Most people think of a blog when they think of content. But there are lots of content mediums your business can use. Podcasting, a YouTube channel, and micro-blogging on sites like Medium are some options.

But how does your ideal customer enjoy consuming content?

How do they want to engage with you?

You want to pick one channel where you can continually build a relationship with your ideal customer. For me that platform is email. For a lot of you, it may be a Facebook group or a podcast.

No matter what that channel is, make sure you capture these people on to a platform that *you* own. And you don't own anything other than your email list.

It's email that gives you more than one opportunity to sell to your audience. It's also email that gives you respite from the changing algorithms social media platforms throw your way.

In the next section, you'll see how to use another core area of your business and a subset of content marketing—email marketing—and how it can help pave the way for your first 100. But have a look at the questions below first. Remember you can download all of these, together with extra resources, in a fillable PDF at **https://yourfirst100.com/bonus**.

ACTION

1. Are your ideal customers able to identify you as an expert in the 1–2 main topics that you regularly share about?

2. If not, what will be your content focus areas? What more can you do so that your ideal customers can easily connect you as an authority/expert in that area?

3. If they are able to identify you as an expert in 1–2 main topics, are they the same areas that you want to establish expertise in? If there's a disconnect here, what can you do to make it align?

4. Are you doing enough so that new potential buyers can "know" you?

5. Do you have content for each of the different categories that your ideal customers may be in? If not, what content can you add to bridge the gap?

6. Does your content tone/voice align with your brand attributes and brand personality?

7. Is there a gap between how you view your content and how your audience views or experiences your content? If there is, what do you need to do differently so that your audience feels more of the emotions that you want them to feel about your content (e.g., write more or less of a certain type of post, adjust your tone, etc.).

SECTION 3
Email Marketing That Paves the Way for Your First 100 Repeat Customers and Loyal, Raving Fans

My husband and I were looking for a car back in 2016. After scrolling through a bunch of car review sites, calling a few car dealerships, and comparing prices, we had one model in mind.

And guess what?

We started to see it everywhere on the roads, in the newspapers, when we went to pump gas. We just had one thought: "Seriously, everyone drives that?"

Pure coincidence or did we just zero in on the most sought-after brand of the year?

Funnily, it's neither one.

When you're in the market to buy, you're actively looking for information.

You're alert.

It seems as if everywhere you turn, you're finding information about your potential buying decision.

But when you're passive and not in the market to buy, the information can be right under your nose, and you'll miss it.

The same applies to digital products.

Customers are savvy. They will find information about your products and services from their peers, from Facebook groups, from searching blogs and possibly any content medium they can, when they're ready to buy.

But when your audience is not in a "buying mode" ...

When they're not actively looking for information about your product or topic...

You can have the best copywriter work on your sales page, you can even have the best product, but they will zoom right past it.

In his book *Sticky Branding*,[15] Jeremy Miller calls this the 3% rule. He states that only 3% of the market is actively looking to buy at any point in time. But he mentions that there is a huge opportunity in the lower 90% of the market. When you build a consistent relationship with people even when they're not actively looking for your products and services, you become top of mind when they are indeed in the market to buy. They come to you first.

That's where email marketing comes in.

According to the Data & Marketing Association,[16] when it comes to purchases made as a result of receiving a marketing message, email has the highest conversion rate (66%). And for every $1 spent, email generates the highest ROI of $38.[17]

When done right, email lets you capitalize on the mindshare of 90% of your audience in a nonsleazy way. It allows you to be top of mind by displaying your expertise and authority. In this section, you'll discover specific principles and ideas behind email marketing that will help pave the way for your first 100.

7 – INTERRUPT WITH EMAIL

Email has a bad reputation.

It's always been rumored that email's going to die out. About how emails are a waste of time because of the abysmal open rates, spam filters, and the sheer irritation that customers face because of clogged inboxes.

Yet, despite all these accusations, email has survived since the '90s and hasn't shown any signs of fizzling out. It *is* still possible to stand out today in your ideal customer's crowded inbox if your emails grab attention, interrupt, and are relevant.

Here's a scenario.

Let's say you enter a store.

The salesperson asks if you need help with something.

You look up, smile, and say, "Just looking."

We've all been in plenty of situations like these.

Do we scold the salesperson for interrupting our leisurely shopping time? Do we despise her for it?

No, we don't.

We recognize that she's doing her job.

Now, imagine you're in a rush or you need something urgently—you forgot to buy a gift for a colleague's 3-year-old son.

You come into a store with racks and racks of toys not knowing where to look but still having to make that dinner appointment at 7 p.m. In situations like these, that "Can I help you with something?" is a more than welcome interruption, right?

That's how it should be when you're using email to sell your products.

Your email has to be a **welcome interruption**.

People don't mind being interrupted by email. They only mind if the interruption doesn't make any sense to what they think they're there for.

And this is where email becomes a lost opportunity for digital solopreneurs and small business owners. It's beyond the scope of this book to cover the very basics of which email service provider to use or how to get set up with the tech.

I assume you're not someone who says that email is dead, dying, or will die.

You *can* be skeptical about the results of email marketing.

You *can* be confused about how to use it in your business.

But you need to be open to giving email marketing a significant role in your business. You need to take the time to create an email marketing strategy.

Because when you have an email marketing strategy, you'll have more people who welcome your interruption than those who don't.

8 – EMAIL DEAD ENDS AND MISSED OPPORTUNITIES

Some time ago I subscribed to the list of an established blogger.

After clicking the link in the confirmation email, I was sent to a page that simply said, "Subscription confirmed!"

That was about it. I did not get any follow-up email. I was not redirected to another page where I could get the promised download. There were no calls to action as well.

It was a dead end and a missed opportunity.

Are there similar dead ends in your business?

There are two key factors with email—**an invitation and a conversation.**

You're focused on getting a tribe of loyal customers.

For starters, you need to *invite* people who potentially will go on to become buyers.

But how do you do this?

The days of sticking an opt-in form with "subscribe for updates" in the sidebar and still being able to get a ton of subscribers are gone. That used to be novel about seven years ago. People today are inundated with subscriptions. I bet you have subscriptions to multiple email lists as well. (And if you have a "subscribe for updates" form on your site, let's keep it hush and fix it soon!)

The best way to invite your audience and the first step in growing your email list is to offer a lead magnet or an opt-in incentive. This is a crucial component of the premier (first) touch point.

But what do you offer?

This is where you could look back six months to a year before and reflect on what a terrible mistake you made.

Here's what you're often told: create a lead magnet that addresses your target audience's pain point.

Fair enough. But it does seem like finding a needle in a haystack, doesn't it? How do you know what pain points to look out for? Your target audience may have issues with so many things, but what lead magnet would work for your business as well as for your target audience?

Imagine creating a lead magnet that does amazingly well but ends up attracting the wrong audience? Or worse, gives them the wrong impression about who you are and what your business is about.

Here are some attributes that a robust lead magnet should have:

1. It's easily consumable

Your readers are already suffocating with information. They don't want a long 30-page e-book. Your lead magnet should be something they can consume quickly and then take action.

2. It's highly specific

Your lead magnet should be highly specific to your target audience. A strategic lead magnet attracts the right people—people you can prime and who are interested in what your business has to offer. It keeps people who are not your target audience out of your email list. Your lead magnet should not and cannot be for everybody. You can nurture a list of 10,000, but if only 500 people are even remotely interested in what your business has to offer, you've just wasted all your time, money, and resources attracting the other 9,500 people.

3. It provides a quick win

Your lead magnet should tell your audience how to do something or outline a process quickly.

4. It leads your audience through a change

Every piece of content on your website should bring your audience from A (their current state) to B (their desired state). Your product and your business's core message should sell a "change." The same with your lead magnet. This is a concept that I explore more in The One Hour Content Plan as well.

5. It talks about one idea

Your lead magnet should have one idea or goal as opposed to several ideas.

6. It's different

Are there similar lead magnets in your niche? While similar lead magnets in your niche are a sign that there is a demand for that lead magnet, you also need to know if the lead magnet is in oversupply. Is your niche tired of seeing it?

7. It contributes to your brand, your current product, and your future products

What do you want your brand to be known for?

What products do you have or will you have?

A lead magnet sits at the top of your sales funnel and guides your reader to your paid offering.

It should not be a stand-alone item but rather gel with your products and offers as well as your content.

If someone opts-in to a lead magnet on writing tips, they are raising their hands and letting you know that this is something they are interested in. They probably identify with the need for them to improve in that area. If you nurture them and build trust and then go on to try to sell them an e-book on 50 essential writing tips, they are more likely to buy your product as opposed to if you pitch them an e-book on productivity tips. This subscriber identifies with the problem your lead magnet solves and hence will be more likely to buy that related product compared to someone who doesn't.

Alignment is key here.

A lead magnet that's aligned with the products and services you offer will attract someone who can then be primed to purchase from you.

But getting subscribers is just one part of the equation. What's more important is what you do with them next.

9 – STACK YOUR VALUE LADDER

The experience a subscriber has with your emails in the first couple of weeks will set the tone for the rest of their time on your list.

This is where the pivotal touch point comes in. The pivotal touch point often seals what your audience thinks about you.

What do you send your subscribers after they have opted-in?

You may have heard about sending a welcome email to your subscribers. If you're already doing that, great! But you'll be squandering the opportunity to wow them and gain their trust if you only send a *single* welcome email. What you want to do is send a sequence of emails instead.

An email sequence is a series of emails that are sent on auto, based on a frequency and order which you predetermine. Not everyone who comes to your site is going to know how your products can help them from the get-go. And not everyone is going to purchase from you immediately. Only a very small percentage of people will buy right off the bat. The rest of them need to be nudged and educated.

An email sequence presents the perfect opportunity to do so. This is how you optimize the pivotal touch point.

But what goes into a sequence? What do I put in? What should I leave out?

I'm going to flip the question around and ask you: What do you want to achieve at the end of that sequence?

You structure your email sequence based on that end goal.

Here are the steps you need to take to create an email sequence:

State the goal of your sequence

What is the end goal or objective for your email sequence?

- Are you going to ask for a sale for a product?
- Are you looking to turn them into a client?
- Do you want them to join your mastermind?

A sequence without an end goal can end up being painful because your subscribers don't know what to take away from each email and what you're inching them toward.

Now, your end point doesn't necessarily have to be a pitch. It could also be an invitation to join your community, to establish your authority and expertise, or to build trust.

2. Plan how many emails you're going to have in your sequence

You need to ask yourself if you have reason to believe that your subscriber is ready to take action on that end goal that you've set for your sequence. The onus is on you to ensure that they have all the resources they need to make an informed decision at the end of the sequence. How many emails do you need to include for your subscriber to get to that place? That's your magic number!

Half the battle is over once you have Steps 1 and 2 out of the way.

3. Get more people into your sequence
How will your audience *find* or *get into* that sequence? How many pathways into the sequence are there? The more you create, the more subscribers you will have heading toward that end goal.

Offer your lead magnet or content upgrade (which is an add-on or supplementary piece of material to a post) at the bottom of your blog posts in exchange for their email address. For instance, I have five posts on my blog about email lists, each with a related lead magnet. Once someone opts into those lead magnets, they will be connected to an email sequence of educational content about email marketing. The end goal is to get them to sign up for the VIP list of my signature course.

4. Analyze

Once you have a good number of people go through your email sequence, it's time to analyze and optimize that sequence. You want to identify what moves your target audience. You want to give them more of what they like and respond to. You want to duplicate the success of those emails with high open and click-through rates.

The crucial point here is that your email sequence should be a natural extension of the content that the reader has just consumed in the pre and first touch points. The content shouldn't feel like a stretch where you're connecting two extremely different topics together. The alignment of content to opt-in offer to paid product or service pitch is important. This is how you stack your value ladder.

10 – EMAILS THAT HOOK WITH 4C

Now, that you know the power of an email sequence, let's drill down into the type of emails that will help you hook loyal customers. There are four parts to emails that hook.

Credibility

You don't need to be an expert.

You don't need to have a certification or have been in business for an insanely long period of time. You don't need to earn six figures or be an author as well.

You just need to be two steps ahead of your ideal customer.

Are there certain things you did that made you clear your college debt within three years?

Do you save money through meal planning?

Have you visited over ten countries on a limited budget?

What made you start your business?

What experiences have shaped your business?

All of these give them a glimpse of what they can learn from you and what change they can expect from reading your content.

Credibility is a powerful tool that gets your ideal customer to sit up and take notice.

Commitment

Micro-commitments are tiny actions that you get your ideal customer to make, e.g., get them to reply to an email, take a survey, or answer a question.

Yes, you do need to *prepare* your ideal customer to interact with you continuously. Because when they do, they're no longer just passive consumers of the information you send. You can start to engage them by asking a single question in your welcome email. Use this as an opportunity to get to know your audience.

This gets them used to *you* asking.

Now, for this to work, you need to be prepared to reply to their emails.

If they start to realize that their replies or actions are hitting a wall, and there really isn't anyone on the other side, they'll stop. And this is what you don't want.

Continuity

How do you make your subscribers anticipate your next email?

How do you get them to look out for your name in their inbox?

How do you keep them on edge thinking about something you raised?

You can do this by opening a curiosity gap in your emails. Add a dash of tease and intrigue. Tease them in the postscript or at the end of your email with what you're going to be sending out next. Here are some examples of how to do this:

- Do you know that 90% of what people believe about organic vegetables is wrong? I'll tell you what that myth is tomorrow and how it's going to help you cut your expenditure by up to 50%.

- Do you know how long it takes for your body to form a habit? The answer will shock you. Look out for that tomorrow.

I'm, of course, making these up, but you get the overall idea.

When you tease, you also need to ensure that you close the loop in the next email. You want to live up to that tease and intrigue. Don't leave them on a cliff-hanger just to say, "I was joking."

That's the biggest trust breaker.

Context

Why does what you're talking about matter now? They've already made your job easier by opting into a resource to say they're interested. Drill into the topic and convince them further on why it matters to them. Are there any myths they're believing in that they shouldn't? Are there any mistakes they may unknowingly be making? Content is where you get them to sit up and take notice.

Email marketing is a huge topic but just working on what I've covered here will put you miles ahead of the competition and on your way to attracting 100 repeat customers and loyal, raving fans.

But consistency is critical with email marketing. Remember we discussed TRUST in a previous section and how it's like a flame on a campsite?

You have to continuously fan it to get your audience's trust. You can't send an email once or twice and then disappear for weeks. You need to decide on a frequency you're comfortable with and then stick with it.

If you want to learn more about email marketing, I have a free email course you can sign up at http://meera.email/course.

In the next section, we'll discuss products (and offers). The way your products and offers are positioned could very well hinder your pathway to repeat sales. But have a look at the questions below first. Remember you can download all of these, together with extra resources, in a fillable PDF at **https://yourfirst100.com/bonus**.

ACTION

1. Do you have a clear call to action that invites a sign-up to your email list?

2. Do you clearly communicate the benefits of being a subscriber to your list?

3. Do you have a follow-up sequence that nurtures your audience?

4. Do you have dedicated nurture sequences for your offers?

5. Is your lead magnet aligned with your business?

6. 4C—Are your emails lacking any of these components?

7. Does the tone in your emails align with your brand attributes and brand personality?

8. Are you being consistent with your email marketing in the following areas: tone, frequency?

9. Where are other possible dead ends and missed opportunities?

SECTION 4
Digital Products (and Offers) That Pave the Way to Your First 100 Repeat Customers and Loyal, Raving Fans

Your product – Your offer. They are two different entities.

You may be using these words interchangeably, but there's a difference between them.

An offer is like a package.

It's how you present it.

You can pack a cut of meat with plain brown paper. You can pack the same cut of meat with expensive paper, imprinted with a logo that states "Delighting stomachs since 1936."

Which offer looks more attractive?

That same cut of meat just quadrupled in price.

Here's what makes up an offer:

- The most attractive promise or outcome of your digital product that your ideal customer will gladly pay for. Your product can have ten different outcomes or promises. But not all outcomes are created equal. Some are more important in the eyes of your ideal customer. You need to pick the most attractive ones that they will pay for.

For instance, a mattress can be positioned as something to help you get a comfortable night's sleep or to help you improve your posture. Same mattress, two different ways of positioning. But which calls out to your ideal customer?

This is often the big idea behind your product. Copywriter John Forde defines the Big Idea as an "idea that can be sorted, absorbed, and understood instantaneously." The big idea determines the narrative of your product and is the thread that runs through your pre-launch material, sales page copy, and overall promotion.

The bonuses you offer with your product

- The urgency factors that nudge your audience toward the sale

- The unique value proposition that a buyer can get from your product that they can't get elsewhere

- The hook you use in your copy to drive the sale

A great product can fail with a lousy offer. A great offer can make even the worst of products sell. I definitely don't recommend going this route. A bad product could very well result in losing the trust you have built up with your customers.

In this section, you'll discover specific principles and ideas behind offers that will help pave the way for your first 100.

11 – GIVE THEM WHAT THEY WANT AND WHAT THEY WILL PAY FOR

Harvard marketing professor Theodore Levitt said: "People don't want to buy a quarter-inch drill. They want a quarter-inch hole."

Heard of the drill and hole analogy?

What's the real reason someone will be motivated to spend money on your product?

People buy things because they solve a problem. Look at your offer through your customer's eyes. Do they immediately understand how your product makes their lives easier?

They're not buying the drill. They're buying the hole that helps them convert that dingy basement into an additional storage space.

You're not selling the hole or the drill but the result or outcome.

Your ideal customer wants something that helps lead them to a desired outcome.

It works with everything you offer an audience.

People want extra credit during the holidays because they want to buy gifts to make their family happy. People want to buy a Rolex because they want to feel like they belong and for their peers to look up to them.

So always start not with what you want to sell but what your ideal customer wants to buy to fit their needs.

The most common underlying drivers behind why people buy are to
1. Save or make money
2. Save time
3. Increase emotional benefit/feel better
4. Ease pain, suffering, or negative emotions

Think about how your offer fits into one of these drivers and focus your efforts there.

List out all the possible outcomes that your product could potentially lead your ideal customer to. Then measure their importance against what your ideal customer will be looking for. Not all those outcomes are going to speak to them.

Just like burning in a single-minded brand identity into everything you do, your product should also hit on the single most important outcome to your ideal customer. The outcome or promise of the offer should get them to sit up and take notice. It should disrupt their attention and push your offer from a "nice to have" to a "must have."

12 – HOW TO CREATE LESS BUY-ING RESISTANCE

Ever been in a state of hyper fandom?

You go to a blog and binge read all the posts. Or you have a sudden interest in a topic, and you get your hands on as much information as you can. You don't mind buying some paid resources too.

I know exactly when a new fan arrives.

They subscribe to my list, go on to buy my email marketing template pack and then my Amazon book, as well as my planner.

This person buys multiple products from me over a span of a few days and even drops me a note to tell me how ecstatic they are with their purchase.

They're eager, excited, and ready to immerse themselves deeper into my content.

But in order for that new fan or subscriber to buy, you need to create a painless, low-risk offer.

These low risk, micro-commitments are called loss leaders or trip wires.

These are small-ticket items that you offer your subscriber usually upon opt-in or early on in your email sequence. The idea isn't to profit from that product but to quickly turn a subscriber into a buyer. Because people are more likely to open their wallets and purses for you a second time if they've already crossed that first sale hurdle.

But there are two mistakes here that you may potentially be making.

Firstly, you make the first wall so high that people can't get a taste of your paid products.

Let's take a $297 product and a $39 product.

If the only product you have available is $297, it's going to take you several days to turn a new subscriber into a buyer. Not many people will be comfortable parting with $297 to someone they just got acquainted with. This means a longer period that you have to nurture that subscriber.

Sure, they may eventually be ready to purchase that $297 product, but you can't deny the resistance it creates. But a $39 product creates lesser resistance and is likely to turn a subscriber to a buyer faster.

Secondly, you may be hesitant to offer something for sale to someone so early in the relationship.

That was me. I was irked by the idea of offering a trip wire to someone who had just opted into my list.

So what changed?

I started to view it from the buyer's perspective.

I'm not an impulse buyer. But when I'm sold on someone's free content, and it blows me away or gives me light bulb moments, I don't hesitate to buy that very day I get acquainted with their brand, especially when the offer is a small-ticket item.

Some people are ready to turn from a subscriber into a buyer all in a single day.

They may understand better how your product or service can help, and they are ready to act on it. So why not present your offer to someone who is ready and willing to take that first step in the relationship?

Look for more opportunities where you can get readers and subscribers to experience your paid content. Because once they do and they enjoy it, they will most likely buy from you again.

13 – CREATE A PRODUCT ECOSYSTEM

This is a book about getting repeat, loyal customers to buy your products. You don't want them to buy once and then just leave. You want them to add your products to their tool kit. You want them to say, "Yes, I could use that" and "I'm going to come back for that."

For them to be able to repeatedly buy from you, you need to create a product ecosystem.

A product ecosystem is when one product feeds into another.

One product helps them take the first step in getting rid of one facet of the pain point. Once they've done that, your next product helps them get rid of the next facet of the pain point. For instance, my products *The One Hour Content Plan* (1HCP) and the *CREATE* planner both help solopreneurs and small business owners with content marketing.

They feed into one another.

While 1HCP helps you with strategy and fleshing out your content ideas, *CREATE* helps you implement and organize what you came up with in 1HCP.

Different products help to bring a
complete transformation

It's just like crossing a river.

Your ideal customer is on one side of the river, and the full transformation of what your business is helping her with is on the other side.

The rocks that help her cross over are tiny steps toward that big transformation.

A full transformation product is something like "Quit your 9–5, grow an online business, and replace your full-time income in 6 months."

Niche courses are the larger rocks.

For instance, Content Marketing, Email Marketing, Digital Product Creation and Launching, and Social Media Marketing are niche courses.

Tiny Products are the smaller stones interspersed between the larger rocks. These address distinct issues within a niche course. For instance, 1HCP solves a distinct issue within content marketing—how to come up with content ideas.

By splitting your transformation in this way, you're making it easy for your audience to become repeat buyers.

14 – KILL THE CRICKETS

Launching to crickets.

That's the biggest fear, right? There's a simple way to get rid of this fear.

Get your audience to make a micro-commitment. We spoke about micro-commitments in the section on email marketing. But what do micro-commitments look like with digital products?

This is where you get them to sign up for a wait list or VIP list or a challenge related to your offer. A VIP list is a simple page with a sign-up form that gives a sneak peek of what your offer is about. It gets your ideal buyer excited. It creates hype and having them make an effort to sign up is a micro-commitment on their part.

Typical numbers say that 1–2% of your email list will convert, i.e., go on to buy your offer. But it's not uncommon to get 10–20% of your VIP list buying your offer. That's the power of micro-commitment and a targeted list of people. Imagine being able to estimate your sales ahead of time through your VIP list numbers.

15 – DEALING WITH INTERNAL VALUE METERS

People want to feel good about the money they spend and the purchases they make.

People also have a baseline expectation of "price to value" in their heads.

It's not something they can necessarily articulate. But they do know whether it has been met or not. Whether you over or underdeliver on what buyers *think* a $297 course is supposed to contain, makes a huge difference to how they are going to feel about their buying decision post-purchase.

When value exceeds the price they paid, you have a happy buyer. You retain their trust and they potentially go on to become repeat, loyal customers. If the price exceeds the value they think they received, you have a disappointed customer and they lose trust.

But here's a mistake most people make.

They think they can pack massive amounts of information and value in their digital products and price their offers real cheap. That would make your customer happy, right?

Well, not quite.

You can't offer a full transformation and promise that your ideal customer will go from zero to setting up a drop-shipping business and earning 5k a month with a $39 product. For that huge a transformation or change, the price point seems unbelievable.

This is when those nagging thoughts creep in:
It's so cheap for the results it promises
It has to be a low-quality product

The promise of your offer has to be aligned with your price point. That's what matters.

Your offer forms a critical part of the prime touch point. Trust is secured when you meet their baseline expectations. But the real magic happens when you *exceed* expectations.

Always keep this in mind when you're packaging your offers. A failed prime touch point could mean that even the work you've put into the first and pivotal touch points will go to waste.

In the next section, you'll see how your selling practices may be affecting your sales. For now, have a look at the questions below. Remember you can download all of these, together with extra resources, in a fillable PDF at **https://yourfirst100.com/bonus**.

ACTION

1. Do you have impulse products which give a taste of your paid products?

2. What can you add as loss leaders or trip wires?

3. Analyze each of your products. Does each offer give a clear promise or outcome potential customers can expect? Does it align with the underlying drivers discussed in this section?

4. What do you need to change about your offer in terms of positioning?

5. Do you have a welcome onboarding sequence for buyers?

6. Do you provide sufficient support and have sufficient content to address different questions your ideal buyer may have before a purchase?

7. Do you direct them to a "Thank you" page or one-time offer page after sign-up?

SECTION 5
Selling Practices That Pave the Way for Your First 100 Repeat Customers and Loyal, Raving Fans

My first product was a course on email marketing that I opened to beta testers for $39.

It was a five-module course with a twenty-page workbook, templates, swipe files, and tons of resources, as well as access to me. I had been nurturing my email list for a good six months before pitching them this product.

But I still felt like a sellout.

I thought someone would call me out for trying to monetize my email list. That I was nurturing them all this while just to pitch them something. It was one of the most difficult emails I had to send.

Been in a similar situation?

So what do you do to get over this?

I started to take note of the type of selling around me that I liked and that I didn't like.

Anything that made me feel bad, I would take note of so that I would never go down that path no matter how highly converting those emails were.

If this is something you're struggling with, start to take note of the type of selling around you that you like and that you don't. How can you bring that into your own system of selling?

There are people who will bombard you with requests to offer your products or services to them for free, to trade, or take it as portfolio building.

They may call you a sellout even if you've provided value.

But they are not your ideal reader or customer.

These are the people who will most likely never buy from you.

Imagine you need a choke fixed in your sink and you call a plumber. Would you ask him to add the job to his portfolio of projects or take it as experience-building work?

No, you wouldn't.

Likewise, you're offering your time, expertise, or knowledge in exchange for remuneration. So don't apologize for wanting to make a living. But start by showing that you are indeed in business. Having a "Shop" or "Work with Me" page where you list out your products and services is the first step. These send a signal that you are in business.

Lay out clearly who you serve. Call out the pain points of your ideal customer. Treat your work with me page or your product listing page as a sales page. You want people to identify with the product or service you're offering. You want to grab mindshare even if they're not ready at that point in time to buy from you.

In this section, you'll discover simple selling practices that will help pave the way for your first 100.

16 – DROPPING THE OFFER BOMB ON AN UNSUSPECTING AUDIENCE

You show up with your offer one fine day and tell people to go buy it.

Sure, you list the benefits and how the product can help them. You don't sound sleazy and come at it from a helpful angle. But you still won't be able to make up for all those sales you could have made if you had had a prelaunch phase.

What exactly is a prelaunch phase?

The prelaunch phase is critical for a number of reasons:

1. Makes your audience aware that they have a problem that needs to be solved

2. Gets them to view you as an expert and trust you with the subject

3. Gathers an interest list

4. Builds anticipation for your upcoming product launch

The prelaunch phase gets the gears turning in your reader's head.

You're priming them for the "ask."

If your ideal customer is not convinced they need your product—if they have objections that your product won't work for them—then as persuasive as your sales page is, it still won't net you sales.

That's because your ideal customer could possibly be at the very beginning of the customer journey. We discussed this in section 2 on content.

Sending that kind of traffic to your sales page is a conversion killer.

An ideal customer who has no idea that they have a problem that needs solving will not appreciate your solution.

Always consider if you have done enough to raise awareness of the problem that your product is solving, instill desire, and remove objections *before* asking for the sale. That's the kind of traffic that's primed to buy your product and which you should be sending to your sales page.

17 – EVEN A 3-PART VIDEO SERIES WILL FAIL IF...

You can try different launch vehicles—challenges, email course, webinars, lives, or a 3-part video series.

But if hype is missing, you may end up with a lackluster launch.

Here are a few ways you can build hype for your launch:

1. Tell them what you're working on *when* you're working on it not when it's done

This was tough for me. I never like to commit before something is ready and when I don't have all the pieces in place. But I started sharing about my Amazon book when it was 75% done. I also asked my ideal customers to share questions they had about the topic. This helped me think about the way I was framing my offer and if tweaks needed to be made.

2. Tell them the *why* for creating this product

Every product of yours can have a marketing story attached to it.

The more you tell it, the more it sticks.

The more they see themselves in that story, the more they see themselves wanting that product.

For instance, this is a story that I've shared often on podcasts and interviews.

How did **Email Lists Simplified** *come about? It came about as a result of my frustration with what was being taught and the message being spread...that a big list is a magic bullet...an elixir that will propel you to six figures...and why I believed that the money's not in the list...but what you do with it and the relationship you have with it...*

What about **CREATE** *planner...How did it come about? As a full-time blogger, I found myself straddling a notebook for daily tasks, a huge desk calendar for promotions and launches, tracking my analytics in one and planning my content in another. It was confusing and downright frustrating. I tested at least eight planners hoping to find the right one. Something that would merge goal planning and content planning...But nothing quite worked.*

Here are some questions to think about when you come up with a marketing story for your product.

- Why did you come up with it?
- What inspired the creation of it?
- What are the results of the product?
- How does the product look in action?

3. Repeat your message often

You may feel like you're saying the same thing over and over—within the same launch or across different launches of the same product.

That's ok!

When you repeat the message behind your product, it gets stronger.

It also contributes to the branding of the product.

People need to see a marketing message several times before it registers and they understand what the product is about.

There is an art to writing prelaunch content that teases, provides value, and promotes your product at the same time. You need to tread carefully and balance not giving away too much and giving away too little that they can't connect you as being an expert on the topic of your product.

When you balance all three together, you create hype and build anticipation for your product.

18 – WHAT'S NOT FOUND CAN'T BE BOUGHT

You've launched your product. Great!

But how is it going to be found?

Believe it or not, that "Shop" that you have on your navigation bar is not going to get you as many sales as you think.

You could send cold traffic—people who have never heard about you, never tasted your free content, never been nurtured by your emails—to your sales page by paying for ads.

But is it going to be effective?

Not quite.

For every product you have or create, you need to consider if there's a pathway or multitude of pathways for that product to be found. How will people get to that product?

For instance, let's say you have a meal planning e-book that you pitch at the end of an email sequence. The only single point of entry for someone to get onto that sequence is by subscribing to a lead magnet on meal planning tips. And there is only one single opt-in form on one of your blog posts where someone can subscribe to that lead magnet.

How many people do you think you're going to be sending into your sequence on a weekly or monthly basis?

Not many, especially if that post is not highly trafficked.

Have a look at the diagram below.

Potential for traffic you're sending	Content	Opt-in incentive	Sequence type	Product being pitched
	Blog Post A (A sign-up form on one blog post)	Lead Magnet: 1. 10 Meal Planning Tips	Meal Planning Sequence (Goal: Pitch Meal Planning e-book)	Meal Planning e-book
	Blog Post A, B, C, D (A sign-up form on each blog post)	Lead Magnet: 1. 10 Meal Planning Tips	Meal Planning Sequence (Goal: Pitch Meal Planning e-book)	Meal Planning e-book
	Blog Post A, B, C, D (A sign-up form on each blog post with each having a different type of opt-in incentive)	Lead Magnet: 1. 10 Meal Planning Tips 2. Simple Meal Recipes	Meal Planning Sequence (Goal: Pitch Meal Planning e-book)	Meal Planning e-book

The more opportunities you have for someone to sign up, the more people you will have going through your email sequence and ultimately getting their eyeballs on your product. You need to get people in the door first and *then* inch them toward your solution. But if you open your door only a tiny crack, not many people will be able to get in, in the first place.

While more content definitely doesn't equate to better content, you want to create a few key content pieces (with an invitation to sign up for a related lead magnet or opt-in incentive) around the product you have.

You want to keep your product at the center and work outward.

Here are a few other ways you can get your product found:

- Email courses
- Content upgrades that lead to dedicated sequences introducing your product or service
- Pinterest pins that lead to blog posts with an invitation to opt-in to a lead magnet or content upgrade. These are in turn con-

nected to a sequence that leads to your product
- Pinterest pins that lead to landing pages which feature lead magnets that lead to your product
- Guest posts
- Podcasts
- Other paid products where you mention related products

19 – DON'T APOLOGIZE FOR SELLING BUT DON'T "SELL"

Master copywriter and entrepreneur Mark Morgan Ford has three fundamentals rules of selling.

People don't like the idea of being sold to

People love to buy things and shop because that puts them in control.

But being sold to?

Not quite.

You may have encountered salespeople who have cornered you and made you feel icky and uncomfortable while trying to get you to buy. In situations like these, you retreat and the first thing you want to do is leave the store, right? The best buying experiences you've had are probably with salespeople who made you feel happy and comfortable with your purchase. There's no pressure or hard selling involved. You and your needs are put in the center.

The same goes for a digital product–based business. Your ideal customer doesn't like to be sold to. So don't inadvertently become the very sales-person you despise.

Don't ask yourself: Will this product idea sell?

That's the wrong question to be asking. The question focuses on the product, not the offer.

Better questions to ask are

- What other things does my ideal customer want to buy?

- What can I offer that'll help them get rid of this problem?

You don't have to apologize for selling or wanting to make a living. People need to know you're in business too. But always put the spotlight on your ideal customer, not your product. Because if you do, you'll never have to *sell* your offers again.

2. People buy for emotional and not rational reasons

You're often selling to the heart and not the head.

Remember the drill and hole analogy we discussed in Section 4? Get to the root of your product that will appeal to your ideal customer's feelings and desires. Always ask "What's in it for them?" and "So what?" for every feature you talk about in your emails and sales pages.

3. Once sold people need to satisfy their buying decision with logic

Your buyer needs to be able to say, "I made the right decision."

This is where internal value meters which we discussed in Section 4 come into play. Always aim to exceed baseline expectation of price to value in your buyer's head. Support them with content post-purchase. This could be 1:1 support, community support in a group or forum, or an automated onboarding sequence that prompts them to reach out to you for help or guides them through your product. All of these gestures work toward helping the buyer justify his/her purchase.

Asking for a sale is a whole different ball game from asking someone to subscribe to your email list or lead magnet.

It's not easy, and it's a process.

You will fight yourself more than ever, and you will second-guess yourself at every step. After a certain stage, a lot of what stops you is mindset.

But you need to remember that this happens to the best of us.

Every time you make an ask, take a step back after you're done and consider the following:

- What can you change or do differently?
- Can you provide more value or context up front to earn trust before you make the ask?
- Can you tweak your offer?
- Can you experiment with the language on your sales page so that it aligns more with your brand personality?

In the next section, you'll see how to delight your existing customers. Because if people aren't complaining, but they're not singing your praises either, it could mean that you've just delivered what you promised. You're not **delighting** them.

Delight happens when you're tipping the scales and giving them what you didn't promise.

For now, have a look at the questions below. Remember you can download all of these, together with extra resources, in a fillable PDF at **https://yourfirst100.com/bonus**.

ACTION

1. Is it clear where your store or products list is?

2. Is there a clear pathway for each of your offers? Can your offers be easily found by your ideal customer?

3. Do you have prelaunch content for your offers to build hype for your launch?

4. Do you have a clear refund policy to set expectations?

5. Do you actively seek feedback from customers?

6. Is there a process in place to get testimonials from your customers?

7. What is ONE thing you are afraid of trying when it comes to launches and selling your offers? This is something you know will boost your selling, e.g., webinars, Facebook lives, challenges. How can you include this in your next promotion?

SECTION 6
How Making People Your Heroes Paves the Way for Your First 100 Repeat Customers and Loyal, Raving Fans

When every online personal brand is pushing sales emails and affiliate promotions in the face of readers, people are choosing brands that stand out and take the time to build a meaningful relationship with them.

The simple act of engaging and being genuinely interested in your subscribers' responses puts you miles ahead of the competition.

In this section, you'll discover a few ways you can delight existing customers so that they become repeat customers and loyal, raving fans.

1. Ask for testimonials and feedback

Here's why your subscribers' testimonials and endorsements are so valuable.

A recent survey from Collective Bias,[18] an influencer agency, found that "30% of shoppers are more likely to purchase a product endorsed by a non-celebrity blogger than a celebrity. Of that number, 70% of 18- to 34-year-olds had the highest preference for 'peer' endorsement."

This means that your readers are looking for the opinions and experiences of someone like themselves.

So by having testimonials from your own subscribers and customers on your blog, you're far more likely to come across as someone they can trust.

There's no reason to feel uncomfortable with asking your customer for a testimonial if you have reason to believe that you've provided value along every step of the way.

If you think they are ready to purchase from you or to provide you with a testimonial, never fear an ask. I always have an automatic email go out ten days after someone has purchased any of my products to get feedback on it.

Here's a template you can model.

Hi friend,

It's been about 2 weeks since you got [PRODUCT NAME], and I'm excited to know what you thought about the e-book/course/mini-course.

I would love if you could send me a few lines telling me if you enjoyed [PRODUCT NAME], and if it has transformed or impacted your blog and business in any way.

Here are a few questions that I would love for you to answer in your feedback:
1. What made you get the e-book? Were you happy with your decision or was it a disappointment?
2. How did this e-book transform your blog or your knowledge & skill level?
3. How is this e-book different from others on the market?
4. What is one thing this e-book offers that no one else does/teaches...or at least no one else does/teaches as well?
5. Will you recommend it to others?

You can send a video, email, tweet, FB comment, FB message, anything you're comfortable with, and it really doesn't have to be long.

If you wanted something to be covered that you thought was missing, you can give me your honest feedback as well!

Just to say thank you and that I'm extremely grateful for your feedback, I'd love to give you [link or attach free resource].

Just reply to this email with your feedback.

Thank you so much once again!

[SIGN-OFF]

2. Send out "the free consultation" email

The survey or free consultation email is some-thing that you need in your email marketing mix. If you need to hone in on what content to deliver or what product to create, ask your subscribers. Send them a survey in return for a consultation or a free call.

Here's a little tip. Assuming you have been sell-ing to your ideal customer, send the survey out only to people who have purchased one or more products from you.

You want to create a product ecosystem as we discussed in section 4. You want to create con-tent that nudges them toward that transfor-mation that your business helps them with. The opinions of your repeat customers matter the most because the insight you get into their prob-lems and what they need help with next is price-less.

Here's a template you can model:

Hey [FIRST NAME GOES HERE],

Could you help me with something?

I'm trying to better understand the type of content you're looking for and what exactly you need help with.

Do you have 3 minutes to help me out with a quick survey?

Most of the questions are multiple choice, and I promise the survey form doesn't have a clunky interface. I know how horrible those are.

Your feedback will really help with the type of guides and mini-courses I put together for you.

[SURVEY LINK]

I'd also like to help 5 (or more) of you who answer the survey with a 30-minute session where we get on Google Hangouts or Skype. I can help you answer specific questions you have about your blog strategy, email marketing, or writing blog posts.

If you'd prefer to do email instead, that's totally fine too.

You just have to pop in your email address and blog URL (if you have one) in the survey form at the end.

If you don't have anything you need help with right now, that's ok. You can just leave that section blank.

Within the next 2 weeks, I'll go through everything, pick 5 (or more) depending on the responses, and notify you via email.

What's the catch?

There's none. If you're familiar with the stuff and emails I send out, you know that's not how I work at all.

You can be assured I'm not going to pitch you anything.

Thank you so much, [FIRST NAME GOES HERE]!
[INSERT SURVEY LINK]

3. Identify your repeat customers and surprise them

One of the most effective means of making your customers happy (and turning them into repeat, loyal customers) is to surprise them.

Keep a system where you regularly identify engaged subscribers and repeat customers. Tag customers who have purchased from you within your email service provider. By identifying them, you can send them special offers, beta test opportunities, or solicit feedback. You know they'll be more likely to respond with comments. They'll also appreciate that you reward them for their loyalty and for doing business with you.

4. Make them feel special

Take an interest in their lives and families. Drop them a note to see how they are doing. If you make a genuine effort to respond to their emails, you will make a lasting impression on them and show you care.

You may not know all your subscribers. But there are names that you'll start to be familiar with—who have written to you and have taken an interest in your work.

If you notice their work on any Facebook promo threads or on Twitter, make it a point to like their post. It's a lovely gesture, and people will feel special that you've noticed them.

8. Offer a referral/affiliate program

Don't offer affiliate opportunities to just your peers but also to subscribers who have purchased your courses or products.

A referral scheme can help you achieve two key goals:

1. Acquire new customers

2. Turn existing customers into brand advocates

But for any affiliate and referral program to be successful, you need to provide support in the form of email copy, images, and social media text.

The more support you provide, the easier it will be for them to know how you want your product or service promoted. Then take an extra step and promote your subscriber/customer reviews and posts as you would your own.

20 – WHAT YOU FAIL TO DO AND SAY MATTERS

While I've given you suggestions on how to build a better relationship with your existing customers, what you fail to do and say matters more.

Have you heard of the term service recovery policy?

Most companies have one.

It's a protocol or internal manual of sorts that staff can refer to when there are lapses in their service, when customers complain, or when their brand fails to meet promised customer experience benchmarks.

But in the online space, many businesses don't have one.

When your product fails to deliver...

when a download doesn't open...

when a paid product never arrives...

when an email sequence doesn't go out...

when you miss your deadlines...

how and *what* you respond matters.

Equally as important is what you *failed* to say.

An apology and follow-up when there should have been one. An explanation of what went wrong and how you're going to make it better. Remember that people will value and pay for the way you make them feel. So make it count.

ACTION

1. Are you keeping track of who has purchased from you? If not, what can you put in place to tag these people?

2. What ideas do you have to delight your existing customers?

CONCLUSION + NEXT STEPS

In the last few sections, you discovered how the 5P Touch Framework helps you create a consistent brand experience for your ideal customer.

You also drilled down into each of the five core areas—branding, content, email marketing, products and offers, selling practices—and how they feed into the 5P Touch Framework.

You're armed with some powerful ideas of what you could potentially do within each of those core areas so that you build a business that attracts 100 repeat customers and loyal, raving fans.

You're also in a better position to analyze where you currently stand with each touch point—where you stand with the kind of experience you are giving your ideal customer.

Here are some questions for you to think about right now.

You may have already been taking notes on paper or a word processor. Or you may not. I urge you to put your thoughts down on paper or type them out. Putting your thoughts down on paper or seeing them on a screen is totally different from housing them in your mind.

1. Write down all the ways your customers have contact with your brand across the 5Ps. Here's how it could potentially look for you.

Pre-Touch Point	Premier (First) Touch Point	Pivotal Touch Point	Prime Touch Point	Post Touch Point
Podcasts	Landing page	Emails	Sales page	Feedback form
Facebook groups	Welcome email		Thank you page	1:1
Blog posts	Thank you page		Upsell	
Pinterest	One-time offer		Support	
	Inquiry form		Facebook group	
	On-site chat		Welcome email	

2. Are all touch points being communicated with the same tone and message? Which touch point is not communicating your brand clearly?

3. Are there any voids, gaps, or holes between the touch points that may cause subscribers or readers to drop off? Here are some examples of what these may be:

- You don't have an invitation to sign up to your email list.

- You don't have a welcome email and send subscribers to a "you are subscribed" template provided by your email service provider.
- Your pivotal touch points are sorely lacking, and you don't interact with subscribers beyond sales emails.
- You don't have a refund policy on your sales pages which makes dealing with refunds difficult due to unclear expectations.

4. Is each touch point differentiating you from others in your niche?

5. Which touch point is the most valuable to your brand? What can you do to improve the experience your ideal customer has with that touch point?

6. With the ideas and principles you learned in this book, make a goal for each touch point as you move forward.

Like I mentioned at the very beginning, 100 is a just a number. Because once you set the wheels turning in the direction of 100, any number is within reach.

Many of the ideas I spoke about in this book as well as the touch point system are not unique.

But what's unique and novel is how they apply to personal online brands selling digital products.

Where do you go from here?

I've raised several tough questions throughout this book including the ones above.

You may see gaps within your business. You may be doing well in certain touch points and not in others. You may not have all the answers to the questions I've raised. But I hope it gets you thinking about your brand in the online space and what you can do to build a better experience for your ideal customers.

The 5P Touch Framework is never just done once.

It's a blueprint that you need to revisit on a yearly basis as your business and offers evolve. It gives you structure and helps you view your business from a macro as well as micro angle. It helps you see things that you could otherwise have missed while you're busy working "in" your business.

Building brand loyalty takes time.

Turning your subscribers into brand advocates takes time.

You have to stand out in that busy inbox.

You have to fight to get noticed.

You have to show them you care.

You have to earn their trust and delight them.

But it's well worth the effort.

I hope you build a business that goes on to delight customers, cultivates trust and loyalty, and makes an impact in the online space.

Before you go, remember to download your bonuses at **https://yourfirst100.com/bonus**.

Good luck and thank you for sharing your work with the world!

THANK YOU FOR READING

I hope you enjoyed reading this book.

I really appreciate your feedback, and I love hearing what you have to say.

Could you leave me a review on Amazon letting me know what you thought of the book?

Thank you so much! If you want to get in touch, come find me here at my slice of the internet: https://www.meerakothand.com.

Meera

MY OTHER BOOKS ON AMAZON

RESOURCES

1. White House Office of Consumer Affairs, cited in 75 Customer Service Facts, https://www.helpscout.net/75-customer-service-facts-quotes-statistics/

2. Marketing Metrics, cited in 75 Customer Service Facts, https://www.helpscout.net/75-customer-service-facts-quotes-statistics/

3. White House Office of Consumer Affairs, cited in 75 Customer Service Facts, https://www.helpscout.net/75-customer-service-facts-quotes-statistics/

4. "Modern Loyalty: Love in a Time of Infinite Choice," *Facebook*, November 2, 2016, https://www.facebook.com/iq/articles/modern-loyalty-love-in-a-time-of-infinite-choice?ref=wpinsights_rd

5. "Modern Loyalty: Love in a Time of Infinite Choice," *Facebook*, November 2, 2016, https://www.facebook.com/iq/articles/modern-loyalty-love-in-a-time-of-infinite-choice?ref=wpinsights_rd

6. Nicholas J. Webb, *What Customers Crave*, New York, AMACOM, October 13, 2016, https://www.amazon.com/dp/0814437818/

7. Adam Richardson, "Touchpoints Bring the Customer Experience to Life," *Harvard Business Review*, December 2, 2010, https://hbr.org/2010/12/touchpoints-bring-the-customer

8. Sue Cockburn, "Consistency: The Key to Building Strong Customer Relationships," *Nimble Blog*, June 25, 2013, http://www.nimble.com/blog/consistency-the-key-to-building-strong-customer-relationships/

9. Brené Brown, "The power of vulnerability," TED Video, TEDxHouston, June 2010, https://www.ted.com/talksbrene_brown_on_vulnerability?language=en#t-406950

10. Kirsten Oliphant, "How to Turn Readers into Raving Fans -051," *Create If Writing*, July 14, 2016, https://createifwriting.com/051/

11. John Hall, *Top of Mind: Use Content to Unleash Your Influence and Engage Those Who Matter to You*, New York, McGraw-Hill Education, April 20, 2017, https://www.amazon.com/dp/1260011925/

12. "The 5 Customer Segments of Technology Adoption," *On Digital Marketing*, https://ondigitalmarketing.com/learn/odm/fou ndations/5-customer-segments-technology-adoption/

13. Brian Carroll, *Lead Generation for the Complex Sale*, New York, McGraw-Hill Education, June 7, 2006, https://www.amazon.com/Lead-Generation-Complex-Sale-Quantity/dp/0071458972

14. Joe Pulizzi, *Content Inc.: How Entrepreneurs Use Content to Build Massive Audiences and Create Radically Successful Businesses*, New York, McGraw-Hill Education, September 8, 2015, https://www.amazon.com/Content-Inc-Entrepreneurs-Successful-Businesses/dp/125958965X

15. Jeremy Miller, *Sticky Branding: 12.5 Principles to Stand Out, Attract Customers, and Grow an Incredible Brand*, Toronto, Dundurn Press, January 10, 2015, https://www.amazon.com/dp/1459728106/

16. Casey Hampsey, "Saturday Stat Series: The Influence of Email Marketing Messages," *Data & Marketing Association*, August 3, 2013,

https://thedma.org/blog/data-driven-marketing/saturday-stat-series/

17. Stewart Rogers, "The State of Marketing Technology Winter 2015: Cost of ownership and return on investment," *Venture Beat,* December 18, 2015, https://users.venturebeat.com/register?ref=http%3A%2F%2Finsight.venturebeat.com%2Fnode%2F886%2Fpreview

18. Colleen Vaughan, "Do Celebrity Endorsements Still Matter for Marketing?" Collective Bias, March 29, 2016, https://collectivebias.com/blog/2016/03/influencer-marketing-update-non-celebrity-influencers-10-times-likely-drive-store-purchases/

Made in the USA
Columbia, SC
26 June 2018